TUGBOATS

by Jeffrey Zuehlke

Lerner Publications Company • Minneapolis

For Graham, the Mighty Mover

Lerner Publications Company
A division of Lerner Publishing Group
241 First Avenue North
Minneapolis, MN 55401 U.S.A.

Website address: www.lernerbooks.com

Library of Congress Cataloging-in-Publication Data

Zuehlke, Jeffrey, 1968–
        Tugboats / by Jeffrey Zuehlke.
            p.   cm. –   (Pull ahead books)
        Includes index.
        ISBN-13: 978-0-8225-6417-1 (lib. bdg. : alk. paper)
        ISBN-10: 0-8225-6417-3 (lib. bdg. : alk. paper)
        1. Towboats–Juvenile literature. I. Title.
    VM464.Z84 2007
    623.82'32–dc22   2007018971

Manufactured in the United States of America
1 2 3 4 5 6 – JR – 12 11 10 09 08 07

Toot! Toot! What kind of boat is this?

It's a tugboat! Most tugboats are small. But they are very strong. They do many important jobs.

This tugboat is tugging! It is pulling a big **barge**.

This tug is called a pushboat. It is
pushing a pack of barges down a river.

A harbor tug is another kind of tugboat.
Harbor tugs help big ships move and
turn in tight spaces.

Some tugboats pull or push big ships.
This tugboat is pushing a big ship.

Oceangoing tugs are the biggest, strongest tugboats. They can sail far out on the ocean. Their job is to rescue ships that are in trouble.

The front of a tugboat is called the **bow**. Why does this boat have tires on its bow?

The tires are like bumpers on a car. They protect the tugboat from getting dents.

The **hull** is the main part of the
tugboat. The hull sits on the water.

Most tugboat hulls are made of hard steel. They must be strong. They get banged around a lot. Pushing big ships is a hard job!

The rear of the tugboat is called the
stern. A tugboat usually has its name
on the stern. This boat's name is the
Cathy Parker.

This tugboat has its hometown painted on it too. Where is this tugboat from?

The parts above the hull are called the **superstructure**. Who works inside the superstructure?

The **crew** works inside the superstructure.
The crew keeps the boat running safely.
Who is in charge of the crew?

The **captain** is in charge. The captain steers the boat.

The captain works in the **pilothouse.**
The pilothouse has many controls and
switches. The controls help the
captain steer the boat.

The captain uses a radio to talk to the crew.

Crew members check a tugboat's engines. Tugboats have huge engines.

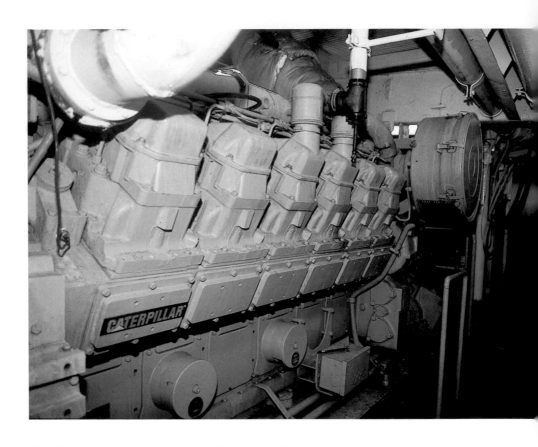

A tugboat need lots of power to do its job. A tugboat gets power from its engines.

The engines power the propellers. The propellers spin. They push the tugboat through the water.

Hey! This big ship needs help getting out of the harbor! Call in the tugboats!

Tugboats can push and pull ships.
They steer ships in the right direction.

Tugboats have to be very powerful to move a big ship. They get the ship out of the harbor.

This tugboat has done the job again!
Thanks for the ride!

Fun Facts about Tugboats

- Tugboats help big ships dock. This is called ship assist.

- Many tugboats have a crew of four people. The captain is in charge of the boat. The chief engineer takes care of the engine and other working parts. The deckhands hook the tugboat to barges and ships.

- Most harbor tugs are between 100 and 120 feet long. That is about as long as seven or eight cars.

- A tugboat's propellers are often called screws because they turn like screws.

- Barges carry food, gasoline, sand, and many other important goods. But barges need tugboats to push or pull them.

Parts of a Tugboat

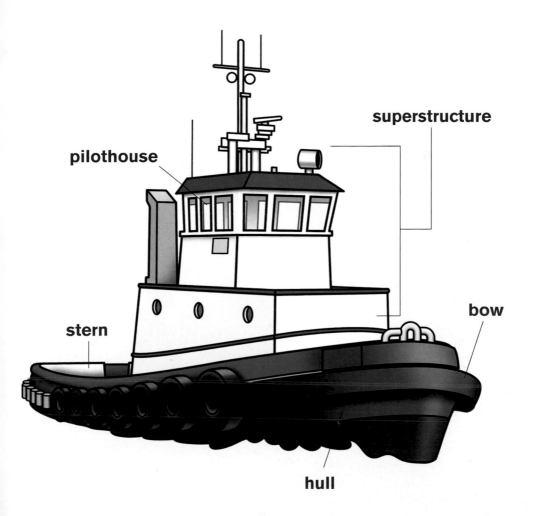

pilothouse

superstructure

stern

bow

hull

Glossary

barge: a flat-bottomed boat that carries large loads

bow: the front of a boat

captain: the person in charge of a tugboat

crew: the people who work on a tugboat. A crew usually has a captain, an engineer, and some deck hands.

hull: the main part of a boat that sits in the water

pilothouse: the part of the boat where the controls and switches are

stern: the rear of the boat

superstructure: the part of the boat that is above the hull

More about Tugboats

Books

Bullard, Lisa. *Power Boats*. Minneapolis: Lerner Publications Company, 2004.

Crampton, Gertrude. *Scuffy the Tugboat*. New York: Golden Books Publishing, 2001.

Lewis, Kevin. *Tugga-Tugga Tugboat*. New York: Hyperion, 2006.

Websites

Northeastern Maritime Historical Foundation
http://www.northeasternmaritime.org/TheFleet.shtml
This website includes pictures and information about several old tugboats that have been fixed up to work like new.

Index

About the Author

Jeffrey Zuehlke has never sailed on a tugboat. But he has watched them chug past on the Mississippi River near his home in Minneapolis, Minnesota. Every time he sees a tugboat, he makes sure to wave to the captain and crew.

Photo Acknowledgments

The photographs in this book appear courtesy of: © Ray Krantz/CORBIS, front cover; © Richard Cummins/SuperStock, p. 3; © Howard Ande, pp. 4, 5, 6, 16; © William Burt, pp. 7, 9, 10, 12, 13, 14, 15, 17, 19, 20, 21, 22, 23, 25, 26; © Stephen Ferry/Liaison/Getty Images, p. 8; © Gary C. Knapp/Getty Images, p. 11; © Bill Ross/CORBIS, p. 18; © Digital Vision/Getty Images, p. 24; © Mike Clarke/iStockphoto, p. 27. Illustration on p. 29 by Laura Westlund, © Lerner Publishing Company.